S0-BAD-141

The Seconds

The Seconds

. . .

poems

. . .

Linda Bierds

A MARIAN WOOD BOOK

Published by G. P. Putnam's Sons

a member of

Penguin Putnam Inc.

New York

A Marian Wood Book
Published by
G. P. Putnam's Sons
Publishers Since 1838
a member of
Penguin Putnam Inc.
375 Hudson Street
New York, NY 10014

Copyright © 2001 by Linda Bierds
All rights reserved. This book, or parts thereof, may not
be reproduced in any form without permission.
Published simultaneously in Canada

Library of Congress Cataloging-in-Publication Data

Bierds, Linda.
The seconds : poems / Linda Bierds.
p.   cm.
"A Marian Wood book."
ISBN 0-399-14786-1
ISBN 0-399-14797-7 (paperback)
I. Title
PS3552.I357 S4   2001   2001019362
811'.54—dc21

Printed in the United States of America

1   3   5   7   9   10   8   6   4   2

This book is printed on acid-free paper. ∞

Book design by Amanda Dewey

Once again, for Sydney

Grateful acknowledgment is made to the following magazines, where these poems first appeared, some in a slightly different form: *The Atlantic Monthly*: "Concentration," "Orbit"; *The Black Warrior Review*: "Portrait of Man with a Lily," "From the Vacuum Tube" (as "Guinea and Feather"), "The Seconds," "'Will You Walk in the Fields with Me?,'" "The Lacemaker's Condenser," "Osteogenesis Imperfecta," "Pasteur on the Rue Vauquelin," "Lister," "Wyeth One: A Midnight Letter" (as "A Midnight Letter of Henriette Wyeth"), "Wyeth Two: Winter Wealth" (as "Winter Wealth"); *Hawaii Pacific Review*: "Dementia Translucida"; *The Journal*: "The Highland," "Anatomies: 1810, 1943"; *Meridian*: "From the Orchard" (as "Curie"); *The New Yorker*: "Testament: Vermeer in December," "The Magic Mountain"; *Third Coast*: "The Last Castrato," "Organmeister: Hasse After Marienkirche"; *The Threepenny Review*: "Latitude"; *Verse*: "Mercator"; *Washington Square*: "Winter Landscape with Gallows."

"The Ponds" and "Grand Forks" appeared originally in *The New Bread Loaf Anthology of Contemporary American Poetry*, and "From the Bayberry Bush" in the exhibition catalogue *About the Bayberry Bush* (The Parrish Art Museum).

I am grateful as well to the John D. and Catherine T. MacArthur Foundation for its generous support.

And again, as always, to Marian Wood.

Contents

· · · *This symbol is used to indicate a space between stanzas whenever such space is lost in pagination.*

Dementia Translucida

●◐◌— PHILIP V OF SPAIN, 1740

My ministers slump through the moonlit halls, wishing
me dead, or at least asleep. In their hands,
wide wings of parchment cackle.

Three times I have exited madness,
as a russet stag exits a pond—a little shaking, perhaps,
while the elements exchange their sovereignty.
And now I am dragging a tepid quill
through jaundiced patches of parchment,
affirming some birth or burning. I love the season

midnight yields, its flat, barely varying
luminescence. Just space and a pulpy loam
defined by striations of night-blooming cereus,
as wax is defined by a royal seal—
all the single-hued peaks and valleys

some wavering hand has passed over.

●◐◌—

It approaches—melancholia—not as a cart
through the palace gates, but
as a distant light in winter.
You remember that ghostly avoidance:

sleighs, perhaps, on the snowy fields, the children
in blankets, and the slender, towering
crownpieces of horses—bells
and the scarlet plumes—floating in moonlight
like flamboyant godlings drawn from three wishes.
Then there, where the village begins, just
there at the side of your eye: a distant light.
Turn, it avoids you. Turn away,
it glows like an autumn pond.

Once I lay six months on my narrow bed.
No bath. No blade. Just my clocks
and the tight-fitting sleeve of my room.

We sat with our various pulses—the oval and boxed,
the jeweled and gilded, the weights, escapements,
pallets and balances
all pulling their cyclic
citizenry. Near my elbow, a diminutive swimmer
stroked the clepsydra's pale bay, pointing the hour
as the tides rose, his hand and tunic

. . .

immaculate, the perpetual silk immersion renders.
And all through the room, on the tables
and walls, little doors introduced their orioles,
and the pinions clicked, and the skaters

circled an icy mirror. My favorites
stood at the window: an indigo globe,
etched with the planets and stars, then
cinched by a band of passing days.
And just to the left, a crystal box,
its pendulum bob a woman, prone
in her red cloak, slicing
the air like a full-bodied figurehead.

Time tossed and retrieved her shadow, again
and again, out over Polaris and a distant Mars. . . .

●∞—

Six months. Then in through my window or wall
a voice began—not child, not man—a castrato's unwavering
luminescence. All the clock-works midway
to their pageantry, and there at the doorframe or sill,
an aria from Hasse:

. . .

.

The sun is pale,
the heavens, troubled . . .
I tremble before my own heart.

Then something of ice and liberty, then the notes
of a minuet. And over my chest and throat and skull
the elements shifted, began their exchange.

They would say, the Chinese, I was healed
by sound—like a mulberry-scented smoke
crossing there and there, through the body's unmarked
vestibules. The Chinese,
who saw time as a knotted rope
down which a slow flame passes.

●☙⌁—

I love his voice.
And then his words.
And then his words' frail cargo. . . .

Near my bedside now, a deep-sided, three-masted caravel
ticks. Gilt copper and brass. Six hand-spans,
bow to stern. At the upright moment

its world begins—which is ours, a second
to ours. Where planking swallows
the mizzenmast, a moon-faced clock chimes.

And out through the crow's nests and portholes,
on the brassy sheen of the decks, a dozen figures
rhythmically turn. And one—the one I imagine
my stand-in, or I for him—slips

through the forecastle's thin door. In his hand
a scepter of oakum flickers. His job
is to seal what enfolds him. To seam
into seamlessness, he would tell you, one must
unwind the given. And so he continues,
rope to oakum, to those downy, primary fibers
that hourly flicker, weightless as souls.

Each night, as I rise to my inverted day,
my castrato sings one aria's notes, year after year.
As the oriole does. I am soothed by their flawless
repetitions, and enter my day

content as the caravel's deckhand—each of us watching
his wide domain, there at our forecastle's door.
Each of us humming some heavenly song,
as we lift and lower our wooden arms. . . .

Portrait of Man with a Lily

●❀❀— AFTER THE MINIATURE
BY HANS HOLBEIN THE YOUNGER

Through the window, winter,
black oxen slumped in the pastures. Someone's whistle,
then the chatter of wagon wheels as, carriage
by carriage, some king or black-eyed queen
bobs through the countryside, outrunning the plague.

In the clouds the ice storms gather. Cold sun
tints the ground to the roan of peaches.
And in a silk tunic, Hans Holbein studies

immaculacy: the dust-free room, the lint-free silk,
his wrists and lye-washed hands. Then he strokes
to the back of a playing card—some king
or flat-eyed queen—a tinted ground.

And waits, powders an eggshell, a peach pit, a stone
from the gall of a black ox. Waits. Sits
at the window, where high on the hillsides

dusk's pandemic wash
darkens the carriages, the clouds that offer

their white petals to the darkening province
of space. Until only a clatter

remains—wagon wheels, ice—as he bends
to the card, outlines in miniature
a swath of cloak. Then smaller still,
a placid, wide-cheeked, tentative face.
Then smaller still, a lily.

Organmeister: Hasse After Marienkirche

They gleam like ribs of a slaughtered hart,
the pipes: prinzipals, dulzians, zimbels.
Just a staggered silence, before stops start

and my father's black boots on the pedals
restore each spectral exhalation.
Sweet ghosts now, all—his pipes more symbol

than symphony, his midnight visitations
more smoke than sound. . . . The doctors warn my lungs
have stiffened, each restless exhalation

spectral in its promise. My breaths predict some
darker weight, they say, the way the rattle's clap—
sharp sound across the smoky cobblestones—

anticipates the leper. Or harness lamps
the horse. I am told the dark owl's silent flights
announce the vole's rattles, though for the way-racked

vole, I fear, that taloned, silence-summoned weight
calls forth a weightlessness—as the slaughtered hart
calls forth a salient gleam, and my father's dark boot
that exhalation when all the stopping starts.

Mercator

Crow, he thought, not goose. The goose, clacking, fattened
to a waxy bulge, submits a quill too bountiful
for the eyelash inkings of continents,
for whale spume and longitudes,
caravels, the Italic hand, the rims
of wind-puffed cherub cheeks. And so,
for sixty years, he dipped into an alum bath—and peeled
and pen-knifed, and polished to a pearly glow: crow.

A bearded man. In love with squid ink.
The sheep-scent of parchment.
The opalescent barbs of crow. In love
with the sperm- and spore-cast *temporal*, although
from time to time, he turned his gaze to *mineral*
and fashioned there, in bronze as cool and foreign
as the stars, astronomers' rings and astrolabes, and once—
blown crystal etched with Pisces, Sagittarius—

a walnut-sized celestial globe.
A doubt-filled man. Six children. Gout.
Imprisoned once for heresy. Yet placid,
mild, a steadfast breath across the latitudes.

Until, one spring, apoplexy sketched from scalp to toe
a centerline, erased to numbness on its western side
his shoulder, arm, leg, hand. Twice daily then, one daughter,
or another, rubbed into his absent limbs an oxblood salve,

while he resumed his questionings: the transient earth,
the endless, frozen arc of stars, like some metallic,
disembodied cowl. How, placed once upon a balance scale,
the ink-filled quill and small celestial globe
were equal in their weightedness. The known
and the unknowable. As, twice daily, shadowed by
his daughter's lowered head, his silent hand and restless hand
weighed equally upon her aproned lap.

From the Vacuum Tube

● ꞔ꞉ꞔ —— TOWARD THE PAINTING *Experiment on a Bird in the Air Pump* BY JOSEPH WRIGHT OF DERBY, 1768

In a carnival tent, near a village square,
on planks purpled by beef blood and a swirl
of velvet show cloths, a crystal tube shimmers,
long as a chimneysweep's leg. At its top, a coin
and feather wait, their brass clip catching the light
as a crowd gathers. And then they are falling together—
the guinea, the feather—through the airlessness,
through the vacuum space the silent crowd
seems almost to increase, each stunned breath sucked
in, in. When they land together on the tube's
glass floor—the feather, the coin—when they settle
simultaneously, someone curses the devil, someone
bites the coin, someone clips it again
in the tube's slim throat, and the falling
continues, guinea and feather, through the seconds
and days, through the decades,
until Wright of Derby pockets the coin, plumps

the feather to a white bird. He has painted
the glass—more bowl than tube—
and the slender pump, the solemn crowd,

one moon at the window, one moon
in the breast of the dying bird, slumped
on the bowl's glass floor. A girl hides her head
in a candlelit hand. A man looks up to an opening wing,
imagines the lifeless weight of the bird
falling on through the airlessness. No papery sway,
no tumble, just head and breast and tail and wing
falling together simultaneously—a movement so still
in its turbulence, he can find in his world no
correspondent: not the wavering journeys of snow
or sound, not the half-steps of dust or moonlight—
and the bird not *beauty*, the movement not *fear*,
although there in the candle's copper light, both
fall equally across his upturned face. . . .

Testament: Vermeer in December

To my daughter, Elsbeth, two loaf-sized, secret coffers.
To my sons, the pastel seascape.
And the peat chest. And the Spanish chairs, perhaps.
And the ivory-capped cane at rest on my bedstead.
And the sheets, and the ear cushions,

and the seventeen pocket handkerchiefs
that flap at the summons of each dawn's catarrh.
Now and then, through their linen expanse
I revisit my children, in flight down an iced stream,
their sail-pushed sleds clicking, clicking,
like a covey of walnut carts. . . .

To my servant, *Bass Viol with Skull.*
The wicker cradle. The ash-gray travel mantle.
To the men who will carry my coffin,
glass flasks—six—and a marbled flute

carved from the wing bone of a mute swan.
Its music may offer a tremoloed solace
as they lift from the gravesite my infant son.
Two years in the earth, his wooden box, darkened

by marl and a bleeding silt, will ride
my greater other like a black topknot
as we are lowered in tandem down the candlelit walls.

To my wife, the yellow jacket, silk and fur-trimmed,
that warms, through the mirror of a linseed wash,
a hazel-haired woman eternally lit by a pearl necklace.
She carries, with a dabble of madder and burnt ocher,
the wistful, enigmatic gaze of my children

as they circled the pale flute, dreaming they said of some
haunted voice, deep in a gliding wing, its song
both shrill and melodic,
like the cry of an infant controlled by a choir.

And to you, in half-rings around me, your faces
spaced like pearls . . . imagine that moment
when the ropes are lowered and something begins
on the lit walls, shape over shape: I leave it to you,
that shadowed conjunction of matter and light
that flies, in its fashion, between us.

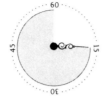

Winter Landscape with Gallows

●℃⌒—— HENDRICK AVERCAMP, 1634

Dusk. And the last sunlight seeps across Kampen.
Somewhere to the west a mill blade bleats, and I
am a child again, near sleep, near waking.
Bent over my small bed, Mother is singing
in half-voice, something of squires and a mottled hen.
She cranks to the left a cotter-pin pole—and there,
the bleating!—as the hammock of rope just under my bed pad
creaks and tightens. I am

Avercamp. Hendrick. From birth, the Mute
of Kampen. But I heard at my bedside
that rude duet—mill blade and cotter pin—heard
through my mother's lips the ruffled shush of
hen wings.

●℃⌒—

From my father's pharmacopoeia, these:

Crab claws. Cuttlefish. Isinglass. Silk.
Oil of earthworm. Oil of ox hoof.
Saliva of a fasting man.

. . .

For a stitch in the side, thistles.
For a blow to the brain, walnuts.
For the jaundiced, turmeric.
For the poxed, snuff.

For the mute,
ivy gathered in a waning moon.

ⴰⲟⲟ—

It began with a weight in the knee.
Then a smatter of stones at the groin.
The plague. Winter. My father stirred
in his long bed, stared at the murmuring surgeons,
their shapes, sheen-edged, like a covey of nightmares:

red leather gowns, slack, prophylactic, the gauntlets
and hoods, each mask with a tapering beak,
like the beaks of the scarlet ibis.

Just a child, stopped in a dark corner, I thought
he was grain for the harpies!

A little ice, now, thickens the window. All morning,
with the strokes of a charcoal pencil, I mimicked
the path of the frozen river, the stall of its ripples,
and the ice, granular,

. . .

like the fumigant salts in the surgeons' beaks.
Aging, how our minds increase their
citizenry! Past joining present,
at the bedside, the door.

●◌◌◌—

It is evening, the table weighted with herring,
dark bread. Here and there, the cellular glisten of
pomegranates, their skins dappled
as a glassblower's cheeks.

Think of bellows, their rigid, tubercular wheeze.
Then breath compressed through a glassblower's wand.
Then the waft of a flat flame.
And there—through bellows, wand, waft:
the unified voices of mutes!

My pallid walls are shadowed by smoke,
a tallow-fed skin that spreads its tint
just to the borders of paintings, mirrors,

as bread will take from the hearthstone chimneys
a dusky rim. A little ale, now. Herring
tart in a salt brine.
In winter, I will be fifty.

. . .

At my father's grave, tallow-fat candles
withered, flared. Twelve, I remember, on the coffin's lid,
like some circular vision of time. Ropes lowered
their fitful light, while the captured breeze
sent shadows, like swallows, there
and there on the wet walls.

●◦◦—

A word written—in ink, or the mist of a winter window—
outlines a deeper clarity.
I have sketched on the fogged pane an *S* and an *S*. Their paths
bleed downward, and now through their sagging frames
a few stars startle!

Eight hundred times
I have crafted the winter landscape.
Charcoal and pen. All the ice-cast gallows scented with
oil. Now and then, I place on a foreground's frozen river
two skaters: a husband and wife, turned from each other.
Not in anger, I think, but awe: just under their feet
the herring are running! And a horse trots
where a caravel sailed!

My couple has found that a mutual absence
increases their presence, as hearing's increased
by the closing of eyes. And taste. Touch.

As vision's increased by
a soundlessness.

⬤⌒⌒—

These are my sounds:

Tisk. Twirr. Three strata of pitched whistle.

My voice in song?
The wavering torches of skaters.

⬤⌒⌒—

And these are my years:

Rowboats. Their tapering hulls.

Frozen half under the river, suspended
just at the crossroads of immersion
and emergence, the arc of their weathered wood
becomes in oil a skater's cape—dipping, aloft—
or the bank of an amber sleigh, one airborne blade
gleaming. Then I draw on the eastern shore

gallows, gibbet and wheel, four onlookers, one hanged body
slim as a stork. I give to his sleeves

a ruby cast, to his collar
the granular texture of
fumigant salts.

Then sky. The vee of three geese.
One windmill's crosshatched wings . . .

The path of the gallows rope
echoes a windmill's bleat, as it saws at the crossbar
and sends to the corpse a slow rotation, back,
forth, some circular vision of time.

I sleep in a bed with a length of cord
tightened by cotter-pin poles. It holds me, just
at the cusp of flight and submergence. As it holds
in its pale braid
a skater's cape. And a coffin's path. And all
down its taut length, holds
the hanged man's emptying shape.
Just at the cusp.
As a cord, I am told, holds the lost word.

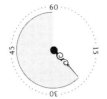

The Seconds

CLAUDE LAURENT, GLASSBLOWER, 1850

With a flurry of sidestrokes, the March wind
swims down the chimney, its air chafed
by hearth smoke and bacon. It is sunset,

and high on the inglenook shelf,
a gauze of crystal flutes
captures the lamplight. I am their maker—Laurent—
eased back in a soft chair, listening

to hearth logs sag through the andirons.
And thinking of seconds—first time, of course, then
the hapless devoted who step from behind
with their handkerchiefs and swords, ready to give shape
to another's passion, as a body gives shape to a soul.

When the handkerchief crosses the damp grass,
they must wish it all back, the seconds:
that the handkerchief rise,
flap back to the hand, and the passion
pull back to its source, as the sword and the pistol
pull back to their sheaths.
Then everything silent, drawn in by some vast,

improbable vacuum—
as an orchestra of ear trumpets might silence a room!

Now the wall clock taps. Across my knees
the house cat casts her rhythmic thrum.
Once I lifted a flute, some second
blemished by a loll in the lime, and blew
through its crystal body a column of pipe smoke.
I remember its hover just over my chest,
a feral cloud
drawn down and bordered, it seemed
in that evening light, not by glass
but by itself.

Seconds and smoke . . .
Into what shape will our shapelessness flow?

Outside my window,
two children bob in the late light,
walking with their mother on the furrowed fields.
They love how their shadows
are sliced by the troughs—how, over the turned rows,

their darkened, elongated shapes
rush just ahead in segments, waving
their fractured sleeves. Now their mother
is laughing, lifting her arms and pale boot,
watching her sliced and rippled

shadow—whose parallel is earth, not she,
whose shape is taken not by her, but the cyclic light

her shape displaces. Now her head,
now her shoulder,
now the drop of her long coat

have stretched to some infinite black bay
pierced by the strokes of a black swan.

"Will You Walk in the Fields with Me?"

EARLY DUELING CHALLENGE

They are matted with frost
and a porous cloth that is the season's first snow.
The fields. The seconds.

And the firsts, of course, their manored lords.

Seen from above in the dawn light, the burgundy,
snow-dappled cloaks of the lords
are two cardinal points of a compass,
its jittery needle defined
by the segmented footprints of sixteen paces.

It is the moment after turning. No one has fallen,
one bullet passing through a hat brim, the other
entering a birch tree with the sound
of a hoof through shallow ice.

At their fixed points, the lords wait. Winter wind
sails through their cloaks. They have entered the dawn
carrying no more than a *sense of self,* the magnetic pull

of decorum, and stand now, smiling a little,
satisfaction obtained by a hat brim,

by a birch that shivers in the early light, as

the seconds do, stomping in place in the snow.
They have entered the dawn carrying, in fact,
two bladders of salve, tourniquets browned
by an aging sun. No selves at all, they
are empty, waiting to be called, waiting to step forth
in another's image—the hat plume and cloak,

after his likeness, the footfalls and trembling. Waiting,
with his grace, to make their turn,

while deep in the dawn's new day, a little
circle of darkness draws a heart-high bead
and the beasts of the fields stand steaming.

Osteogenesis Imperfecta

MICHEL PETRUCCIANI, MUSICIAN, BORN 1962,
DIED OF "GLASS-BONE DISEASE," 1998

Picture a horse on a shallow path,

the thwick, thwick of its hooves in the grass.
That is the sound of the spine collapsing.

Not a pop, but a rasp, he would tell you,
Petrucciani. Evening, perhaps, a gloss
on piano keys, flute, the metronome's

serrated tip. And perhaps he would speak
of a sudden freeze, an orchard shadowed
by a dozen men, long aprons black-waxed
and flapping. Another place, another

century. Reaching deep in their leather sacks,
they are casting water to the vivid limes,
their arms alive with the bow-strokes of cellists.
Then over the fruit an ice begins, dries
into glassy arcs. And over the ice,

. . .

the dark harp of a thrush's song, and over
them all, the weather. And how perfect
the brindles of ice, he might say, curved like ribs
to those greening hearts. Perhaps he would shift
in his soft chair, weight too great on his glassy bones,

his slowly eroding frame, and ask you
to picture the orchard at dawn. One horse
at rest near the frozen path. Now the thwick, thwick
of apron flaps. Far off to the east,

the slow, equatorial rim of the season
widens. Imagine how fiercely they dip the cups,
the lift of their arms, the falling,

how the horse's throat-deep, rhythmic sighs,
and the vapory mist of each dipper's breath,

step forth, take their shapes, and are gone.

The Lacemaker's Condenser

In this amber and aberrant light,
the painting in shadows on the staircase wall
is reduced to a study in fence slats—
an improvement, I think, on its daylight donation
of sheep and a yellowed barn.

We are sisters, making lace. Not twins by birth,
though yearly our distance erodes
and we shift a bit, as the coins of a spine,
I am told, shift closer
in their vertical journey. Should you look

through our window in this April dusk,
we would offer a portrait thickened by symmetry:
from the left, one woman, one water-filled
globe, one broad-based, burning candle.
Then everything repeated, right-handedly.

The globes are a limpid glass with the span
of early melons, and cast to our lace-filled laps
two beams of light, yellow and singular,

condensed on the stitchwork like egg-shaped ponds.
From your stance near the mallow hyacinth,

we must look, in these steady beams,
like Apostles hallmarked by a grateful Heaven,
light in prisms on our nodded heads.
At your window, now,
the moon has emerged from a shallow rain

and casts to my apron and pale shoe
the lengthening shadows of raindrops. I love
their silence and stippled flight, as I love
the alliance the globes permit,
a fusion made perfect by

celibacy. Quite enough to ask
of fire, water, each in its separate domain—
that the candle's glow on the cloaks and hearth
be drawn, down and down into
perfect O's, like the startled mouths of tulips.

Lace is from Latin's noose, I have learned.
And this sinewed length of background thread
is a *bride*, to which the dips and whorls are wedded.
A *bride*, whose crossings are *ground*, deflowered, bare
as the seam one follower threw forth

. . .

when he parted to symmetry a darkened sea.

●℃℃—

She has placed you, I fear, near a hyacinth branch
with the rain already warm in your cuffs.
You must hear at your back
the asthmatic wheeze
of wind through the hedgerows

and the hiss of the lamplighter's torch.
She loves, she has told me, the egg-shaped ponds
condensers yield. I love
the pond-shaped eggs in their iron pot,
how they canter about when the water boils

and crack, now and then, minutely.
How the minerals and salts, and the water's
hidden, swimming lives,
seep to the thickening egg-white, and leave
on its surface when the shell drops away

a ghostly, pewter filigree—
more lovely than any *we* can master.
We are two, alone in a house whose hanging cloaks
cast the open-armed shadows of penitents.
Although no one has fallen—or even, I think,

. . .

sagged in a shallow rain!
When my sister coughs, her staccatoed breath
troubles my candle, and its errant light
sends a circular flapping to
the ceiling and walls, each time bringing

with it a day from my childhood:
first sun and a brilliant snow, then
an ermine trapped in a rabbit snare, the circular
flaps of its milky body. As I watched,
the glare pulled down to one hairless foot

clenched in the noose loop, one glistening,
umber bead. Then the ermine pulled free,
its light tracks sinking a little, in the sun, the snow,
toe and claw prints lessening. Enough to ask of
fire, water: to hold while releasing. Of the tether,

the ground: to have, and to hold
the slow letting go.
Sometimes upon waking, I sense just under my
breastbone, some cold, interior brilliance, dreadful
with promise. Then the eggs begin in their iron pot.

And the day, like the ermine, gradually darkens.

Pasteur on the Rue Vauquelin

Near the red blade of a furred poinsettia,
just to the left of the stamen cluster, a dragonfly slowly
dips and lifts. In the grasp of its tendril legs
floats a yellow almond, or a child's thimble perhaps, or
some bulbous facet of light. It is dawn. The boy,
Joseph Meister, is sleeping, his necklace

of cauterized dog bites
glowing like topaz. In delirium,
he mumbles of scarves and ale tents, how a jester
thumbs back a tankard's lid, and then—
the snarl of a weasel in a woven cap.

This is the grand hour, light coming toward me
in fragments, as if to prepare me
for its greater flood. . . .

When I was a boy, floods toppled the fence posts
and birches. And once,
I watched at the depth of a shovel's blade
yellow turnips afloat in a tepid sea. Their rocking

sent sets of concentric rings,
and there—three Saturns just under my feet!

Dawn. From my soft chair I am tempering rabies
with injections of . . . *rabies!* And tracking
the path of a yellow light, flower to memory to
a mirror of sky. How it dips and lifts
with its quick sting, synapse to synapse.
How that which invades us, sustains us.

Anatomies: 1810, 1943

Picture a sunlight brilliant as albumen, then
the mauve capillaries of Sardinian streets.
In a darkened, stone-lined room, from wax
tinted with rhubarb and bone-white, Clemente Susini
is crafting a child. Her hair is human
and her left lid's lashes
shadow the curve of her downcast eye.

                                      Her right lid
is missing, and the cheek skin, and the skin
of her small torso—or better, rolled back
to reveal to medical students
that which awaits them. He blinks, bends
to the puffed plum of her heart, to the sea-green veins,
the intricate white nerves fanned like flax
at the stem of her throat,

                               as students will bend to this
wax rehearsal, squeamish at first, then stunned. *So this
is the body's substance, cupped by the body's style*—
near her eardrum, bobbed curls, or there, two waxy skulls
shadowed by their Vandyke beards. And *Such ardent
devotion*—his face at the candle, then the pinprick gasps

as wax collapsed and a needle, heated,
wedded each hair to a milky scalp. . . .

Picture a wind crossing in from the gulf, slipping
north through the century, the child
propped upright now on some institute shelf, and the sun
a colder white. It crosses a harbor, blows through
Blackpool's rubbled streets, where deep in the showrooms
of Louis Tussaud, Epstein's *Jacob and the Angel* waits,
its eight-foot alabaster height
                              glowing like wax.
The figures are upright, two naked, male shapes
pressed firmly to each other, chest to thigh.
Their wrestling night is over, and now they stand
like dancers in some marathon that surely sways above them,
across the shattered streets, behind the blackout curtains.
It's Jacob's turn to rest—head back, eyes closed, arms
slumped across the Angel's circling arms.
                              Among the skulls
and marionettes, among the shrunken, minor purchases,
they glow, shimmer with a longing

that slips a glistened stitch between them—between them all,
in fact, each pair of dancers overhead, each coupled
this and *that*: to bend to a pattern's slow step-close.
To sway, yet persevere. To hold some solid otherness,
and be the last one standing.

From the Orchard

●❀❀— MARIE CURIE, 1930

Now and then in a shadowless noon,
light cast equally on the rooftops and hedgerows,
I think we are one, harmonious voice, one set

of days circling. Then something breaks free—an oriole,
perhaps, sings out from the wall clock's tiny door—
and our singleness returns. The hands
that announce its chirrupings
are slim in their metal mittens,
and cross, recross imperceptibly
as the day ages, and the seasons collide,

and I nod in my soft chair, now a woman at tea,
now a girl in skates on an iced canal, in love
with the tranquil loop it makes, village
to fields and back, while the notes of a dockside serenade

swell and fade with her loopings, in love
with the sunlight and smoky tea, as the oriole chirps
and the hands cross, and she walks with her husband,
and lies in her cradle, and seasons the beef, and laces
the skates, and fishes

with her uncle by a torch's light,
as the weightless, silent, lucent shrimp
rise to the surface like radium.

●◐◑—

How the apple leaves keep closing on themselves!—
each dappled fist curled down across
some shimmer of larvae or puffed cocoon.
And the wind, high in the beech trees,

how it throws, rethrows its arid wheeze!
With the gait of the aged
or very young, I have stepped out
to join their constancy, a little moss on my shoe tongue,
and the sheen of my cloak, ruby or wine,
like the sheen of a severed beet.

In their leper's line, they seem chilled—the trees—
curled down across

those swelling, ice-white beads.
Once, through the smoke of a copper lantern, I watched
an infant tucked under a woodstove. Fierce winter,
her body coated with oil. She seemed to me
just a larval shimmer
there in the basket. Then her hands sprang up

in their jittered waves
and it reached me: the mineral scent
of the fully formed.

With a platter of gherkins and marbled cheese, I would sit
with my husband on a sunken couch, our dormant
workroom intentionally dark, and around us,
on shelves in their shallow jars,
the glowing blue bodies of radium.

They nibble me now, I am certain. In the marrow, the blood.

When the oriole stops its aria—and the minute-hand stalls
between rising and falling—its body withdraws
in an instant of color,
like a scarf snapped back through a wizard's sleeve. . . .

Backlit by sun, my husband's ears
held the rouges of wine, and an etchwork
of delicate veins.
Vat by diminishing vat, we
extracted from pitchblende

radium's light.
Four years, stirring, and my hands, deadened

with calluses, curled to the curve of each stir-stick.
At midnight or dawn, I would wake to the scrape

of their quickenings, to that eerie patter of
grasp, regrasp, when nothing at all fills the grasping.

●C๏๐—

A few clouds, now,
inch their shadows through the orchard.
And the night bats stir.

Often I think of their faces, gothic, ceaseless
as flowers. How the gauze of their opening wings
is strung from elongated fingers. Fingers, extended
to wing bones.

Watched from below,
each floats like a consort of Lucifer:

dark scarf,
dark mass extracted from a wrapping of light.

Such a fluttering, there near the beech trees.
Such nubbled, hell-petaled shapes
drawn forth by the curve of a hand.

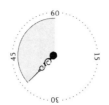

Lister

The Surgery, in the first, empty movements
of dawn, holds the weighted silence a scallop perceives,
with the beach and tide thickened above it.

In a moment, I will scavenge the air
with sprays of carbolic acid. Then the gurneys
will clatter like cattle.

Once, with forceps and knife,
I entered a Lamprey caught in the Thames,
its spine not bone at all—
those minuscule, interlocked
saucers and cups—but a strap of blue translucence

smooth as the world's first sky.
My brother has died, his molars removed
to make room for the swelling. In his terminal days,
he would reach for himself in our glossy mirrors,
or a basin's copper curve. Now and then,

he spoke of a day from our childhood:
a captured stag roped in the cow barn—

how the blacksmith severed its mildewed horns,
the strokes of his blade
like the snores of a terrier.

And the stag then, for hours, throwing back its head
in the stunned submission that is weightlessness. . . .

We covered the mirrors with an eggshell gauze.
Then walked through our garden of cowslip
and the purple needles of rosemary.

Should you place a bell in a vacuum jar, its rings
cannot reach you. Just a sheen
and a slope, and a clapper clacking
soundlessly. The notes, in their swimming, die
at the lip of departure, slip back to some
smooth, translucent, one-seasoned world, cleansed
by stasis—and vacancy.

From our stance in the garden, we watched as my brother
reached out from our hallway mirror,
past the fabric and frame, to the answering reach of
my brother. No sound at all when the mirror shattered,
just my brother and brother, slipping
down and down the wall's cool slope, in a mist
of reflected longing. Until,

with an eggshell gauze, we covered him.

The Ponds

FRANZ KAFKA, JUNE 1924

Always the baths. Although my father in water
was a snared goose—his flappings, then the granular rush
of the foam. No swimmers we, not really. Still,
from the rough-hewn planks of the changing-hut,
we walked in our nakedness.
I remember his girth. Then that sack of quick kindling

that was my chest. And later, long after,
how pond water, warmed from its rest
near the inner ear, seeped out to my pillow slip. . . .

Just a child, my mother had grasped
her grandfather's toes, asked from his fresh corpse
a gram of forgiveness. Ritual, I think, superstition.
All the toe hairs were scoured to black-tipped nubs—
the chafe, chafe of his thick boots—
nubs and nails and a flesh with the chill

of a brookhouse wall. She told me he bathed
in the languorous river, day after day—in winter
breaking the ice with a net of bricks.

And although he brought the water to him, I am certain,
handful by handful, still
he strokes in my mind just under the ice rim,

piece and then piece, as a boiled shirt
strokes up through the vat: now an arm, now the neck,
now a blister of back.

By open car, I have traveled to the sickbeds
of Vienna, then onward to Kierling.
My larynx, they say, has decayed to the flesh
of an autumn berry. I remember

wind through the car seats, how light was slashed
to some rhythmic flick
by the quick interruption of birch trees.
And Dora, her coat held open between me
and the elements, flapping its musk
of camphor and soot.

There is sunlight today. It casts into great herons
the tapering shadows of nurses. . . .

My throat is treated with injections of alcohol—
and my cousin's spleen with injections of milk!
So death, in the body, forms a flaccid pond—or the body
. . .

in death—hourly deepening, stretching down
where lightless ligatures tangle and sway.
Death. In the shade of some changing-hut.
Infinite, black-cast, glacial reach.
And I am buoyed by it.

The Last Castrato

●ᴏ⟩⟩⟩—— 1904

Buoyed by light, the gaping, bronze recording horn
floats near his upturned face, near his lips
that echo in their opaque sheen
the wax now turning at the horn's slim tip.
He is offering Hasse's aria—pale suns in the misty heavens,
the tremblings, the hearts. But the stylus slips
on the low notes and fricatives until only
something like *emblem* remains, a *pale, une'en art*
etching the cylinder's tranquil curl. And so

he is asked to compromise: the lowered tongue, the softened
voice, a forfeiture for permanence. But compromise
has brought him here. And softening. And permanence
has poured its liquid bronze into the gap
the temporary held so steadfastly. He steps away, steps
back. What on earth to do? Encircle loss, finite
and full-throated, as the stylus drops his highs and lows,
his suns and heavens, his seamless climbs from heart to mist?
Or forfeit loss and, so, be saved?

From the Bayberry Bush

●○○○──── AFTER THE PAINTING BY WILLIAM MERRITT CHASE

Just before sunset, he will give to his young daughters
three dollops of oiled white—three brush flicks
straight from his palette to the melted wax

their bayberry berries have rendered. White candles, then,
begin with a wrist flick, one daughter will think,
though the pigment will float on the hot wax, stunned

for a moment, its cumulous shapes sweeping the surface
as the clouds do now, just over her bonneted head.
She is Alice, the eldest, facing her father

in the noon sun, facing his easel and peppered beard,
white pigment still on his brush tip, white berries
still on the bush. Hold, he tells her. And something

quickens within her. For an instant, her brother's face
in his infant's coffin. And the lost twins. Perhaps
they are sun spots, or berries white in the scrub,

those waxed faces flaring a moment, peripherally.
And then they are gone. Her father is laughing, afloat
in his own correspondences—how the house's gambreled

. . .

roof line, high on the painting's horizon, mimics
her bonnet's droop. And the windows
her steady gaze. How the static stirs, he thinks,

and the animate seeps to inanimacy. She is Alice,
his daughter, in a thicket of switchgrass and scruff,
linseed and tint. And now she is crossing

the kitchen floor, while the bayberry candles harden.
How clever, she tells him, that *bay* can be water or leaf.
And a bay's berries . . . like seeds from the sea!

Their fragrance is fugitive, her handbook says, best
kept under cover of glass. And she loves
that what quickens within her then

is just sound and illusion, caught up
in wordplay's sudden wind, as a *fugitive scent*
slips past her, sloughs off its chains, high-steps

through sand scrub and the blackening night.
Not *memory,* not *tomorrow,* standing now in the bay bush.
Just a brush-stroke of fugitive *present,*

both held and released by the branches.

Concentration

We understand the egg-sized ship,
the thread-and-spindle masts, the parchment sails
puffed to a rigid billow.

And the lightbulb that enfolds it.

We understand the man, Graham Leach, his passion for
impossibles. We see him,
tucked within the vapor of his jasmine tea,

while heron-toed forceps slowly wed

a deckhand to a tear of glue.
The rudder would lodge in the bulb's slim throat
but could be folded, slipped inside, reopened

into seamlessness. We understand that sleight of hand

but not this full-sized pocket watch
upright in a 30-watt. Perhaps it's made of lesser stuff
than gold, some nonmetallic pliancy. Still,

it mirrors the museum shelf, and to the left

. . .

the plump barque, static in its perfect globe.
Perhaps he blew a gaping bulb
then tucked the watch inside, rewarmed the glass,

drew out a path, clamped one end's concentric rings,

the contact point's dark star. This would explain
what we've attributed to time
and now must give to fire: the amber face,

the wrinkled Roman numerals—

still fixed, still spaced to mark the intervals
of space, but rippled,
a dozen, ashless filaments. The filament

itself is gone. Gold's light enough, perhaps.

We understand, to make a living bulb,
three hundred wicks were tried. Before a match was found.
Oakum, fishline, flax, plumbago. A coconut's

starched hair. A sprig of human beard.

Three hundred tries, before some agent, tucked
within a vacuum globe, could catch the rasp
outside—that friction-fed, pervasive tick—

and channel it, and draw it in.

The Magic Mountain

To sit on a balcony, fattened by lap robes and a fur pouch,
with the columbines nodding in their earthen pots
and the weighted autumn moon
already casting to the balustrade

a rim of tepid frost, is to know to the bones
the crepuscular slumber of bats—
alit between seasons of dawn and day, day and dusk,
and everything turning, perpetually. . . .

This evening's soup was studded with cloves—
brown pods and corollas—the diminutive heads of sunflowers.
To my left, in a neighboring balcony window,
a young man is dying, face turned to the ceiling,
his red chin beard sparse and pointed. He is joined
by a woman with a parchment fan, although I see only

her hand and cuff, the curve of a damask sleeve.
And a sky of rootless willows, gray, yellow-green,
pleated in parchment, swaying a little as the hand sways,
folding at last to a single stem. And then a sleight
. . .

of magic comes: from the fan's handle
a face is formed, spar by closing spar.
Egyptian, I think. The hooded eyes. The slender beard.
Each spar tucks down to its thin contribution,
earlobe or cheekbone, a slice of brow—
and there! one full-blown, ivory face, perfect
on her damask knees.

Now the bats are aloft, stroking in pairs past the pallid moon.
Once, in the twilit dust of the X-ray room,
I saw on the screen a human lung,
abundant and veined as a willow.

In his bed the young man is stirring, and the woman
has lifted her parchment fan, the ivory face
shining a moment in the facets of lamplight

before its surrender to gray, yellow-green.
And which is the better, I wonder:
To gather from parts such a fullness?
Or to part into fullness so breathtakingly?

The Highland

ZELDA FITZGERALD, 1939

Dear One,

Do you have the time? Can you take
the time? Can you make
the time?

To visit me? The hospital doors have opened to spring,
and its land *is* high, dear one, each slope
with a vapor of crocuses. Its citizens, alas,

are low. Despondent, in fact, though a jar of sun tea
tans on the sill. The woman beside me
has opened the gift of a china doll, an antique
Frozen Charlotte. Glass face, a cap of china hair,
shellacked to the sheen of a chestnut.

At breakfast the shifting returned, dreadful
within me: *colors were infinite, part of the air . . .*
lines were free of the masses they held. The melon,
a cloud; and the melon, an empty,
oval lariat.

. . .

They have moved the canvas chair
from the window. Sun, enhanced
by the brewing jar, threw
an apricot scorch on the fabric. The fruit,
a cloud. The fruit,
a doll-sized, empty lariat.

D. O., into what shape
will our shapelessness flow?

●◯◦—

Dear One,

Italian escapes me. Still, I float to the operas
of Hasse and Handel, a word now and then
lifting through . . . *sole, libertà.* In an earlier time,
the thrum-plumped voice of a countertenor—half male,
half female—might place him
among us, we who are thickened
by fracturings. D. O., now and then, my words

break free of the masses they hold.
Think of wind, how it barks through the reeds
of a dog's throat. How the pungent, meaty stream of it
cracks into something like words—but not. I just sit

in the sun room then, slumped in my fur and slabber,
feeling the wolf begin, back away, then some

great-jawed, prehistoric other
begin, back away, then the gill-less,
the gilled, then the first pulsed flecks
begin, back away, until only a wind remains,
vast and seamless. No earth, no heavens.
No rise, no dip. No single flash of syllable
that might be me. Or you.

D. O.,

Now a gauze of snow on the crocuses! I woke
to its first brilliance—midnight, great moon—
and walked through the hallways. The pin-shaped leaves
of the potted cosmos threw a netted shadow,

and I stopped in its fragile harmony,
my arms, bare feet, the folds of my limp gown
striped by such weightless symmetry
I might have been
myself again. Through an open screen door

I saw a patient, drawn out by the brightness perhaps,
her naked body a ghastly white, her face
a ghastly, frozen white, fixed
in a bow-mouthed syncope, like something

. . .

out of time. As we are, D. O., here
in the Highland, time's infinite, cyclic now-and-then
one simple flake of consciousness
against the heated tongue.

●❧—

Dear One,

My Italian improves:
sole, libertà,
and *Dio*, of course, D. O.! (Although He
has forsaken me.) The tea at the window
gleams like the flank of a chestnut horse. It darkens

imperceptibly, as madness does, or dusk.
All morning, I held a length of cotton twine—
a shaggy, oakum filament—
between the jar and brewing sun.
We made a budding universe: the solar disk,

the glassy globe of reddish sea, the stillness
in the firmament. At last across the cotton twine
a smoke began, a little ashless burn, Dio,

that flared and died so suddenly
its light has yet to reach me.

Wyeth One: A Midnight Letter

●❍❀— HENRIETTE WYETH TO HER SON, N. C. WYETH, 1914

Blue night. And up from the pasture,
wind, then a skeletal trellis of lightning.
Your oils of Stevenson's Jim
support an interior fire. And the foamed sea
near the *Covenant*'s wreck—nine shades of green
and a milky plume—seems lit from within.

Convers, the doctors say I am slain by *longing*—
the illness of Swiss, they tell me: uprooted, brought by boat
to this dappled shore, yearning for . . . edelweiss.
I, who have never seen Switzerland
but through my mother's words, am weakening daily
from its absence! . . .

All morning, with the weightless grace of a sorcerer's carpet,
a fog hovered over the river, one slice of daylight
between them, pierced now and then by a black canoe.
By evening, the village bells were muffled in wind.
Do you know that in warmer seas
shrimp rise at midnight to a torch's light?—little planets

. . .

circling the sun some fisherman holds.
What rises, I wonder, through your *Covenant*'s sea,
lit from above by a brush-stroke of white?

Ah, what gruff counterparts we've become, my son,
taking from others our . . . illustrations!
Now the birds are black in their midnight nests, then white,
then black, as the lightning walks.
Have I told you the mystery of fulgurites?
Lightning petrified into glass rods? Some fusion

of sand and heat, I have heard, then
over a stretch of tawny beach, branches of light
solidify. They must look like the elms of Heaven,
those glittery crooks and jags, those limbs of pure
transparency. Or the ice-blown spars of some alpine flower
held fast in a foreigner's mind.

Convers, if I draw my homeland from another's *words*,
in what region does my longing lie?
Not in the province of Heaven, I think,

or the night sky, or the crystal rod
of any celestial offering—though frequently now
I think of its borders as curved glass,
brittle and thin, like the delicate plates of a shrimp's back,
through which the dark sea's ancient weight
again and again riffles.

Wyeth Two: Winter Wealth

●✑⊸──── ANDREW WYETH TO HIS FATHER,
N. C. WYETH, 1946

Father, with a sweep of his dark sleeve
a boy drove dogs from your drying blood—just a motion,
slow and circular, as if he were stooping
to polish the tracks.

Behind him, a frenzy of crows
turned on the thermals of engine steam.

Your death, they told me, was an instant's click:
first your car, stalled at the crossing, then
all down the track troughs, bits
of batting, flecked glass.
I keep only this: the boy, Allan Lynch,

and the dogs dancing back
from his slow sleeve, from his face
that gleamed between anguish and mercy.

Now the snows have diminished, and the world
turns in its own slow sweep, its own elliptic
fending. Last month, with blacks

. . .

and a yellowed white, I painted the boy
in flight down a winter hill, his cap's ear flaps
eternally lifting, and the hem
of his dark coat. Sometimes I watch

as daily now, he follows his tracks
in the melting snow, heel print
to toe print, as if to regather the body's domain.

Sometimes he tells me his dream—

just red and black and a smatter of white.
At first the colors are ribbons, he says, then
fox pelts, limp in a black barn,
their teeth and eyes like rice.
Winter wealth? he wonders. And now they have stroked

to a boa, thick on his shoulders and neck.
Then he floats, he says, like a dark planet,
held fast in its circles of fire.

Orbit

For warmth in that Swedish winter, the child,
aged one, wore petticoats hooked from angora,
knotted and looped to a star-shaped weave.
And for her father, there at the well lip,
she did seem to float in the first magnitude—
alive and upright, far down the cylindric dark,
with the star of her petticoats
buoyantly rayed on the black water.
One foot in the water bucket, one foot
glissading a brickwork of algae, he stair-stepped
down, calling a bit to her ceaseless cries, while
his weight, for neighbors working the tandem crank,
appeared, disappeared, like a pulse.
In bottom silt, the mottled snails
pulled back in their casings
as her brown-shoed legs lifted, the image
for them ancient, limed with departure:
just a shimmer of tentacles
as the skirt of a mantle collapsed
and a shape thrust off toward answering shapes,
there, and then not, above.

Latitude

With a framework of charts and reckonings, reason tells us

they died from time, the rhythmic tick of hub and blade
that, turning, turned their fuel to mist.

And reason says, while Earhart held the plane

balanced as a juggler's plate, Noonan tipped the octant
toward the stars, and then, no radios
to guide them, toward the dawn and rising sun.

On the hot, New Guinea runway, they'd lifted glasses,
a scorch of mango juice brilliant in their hands.
Around their heels, a dog-sized palm leaf fretted,
then the cockpit's humid air slowly chilled to atmosphere
and there was nothing: two thousand miles
of open sea, theory, friction, velocity. The weighted *ifs*,

the hair-thin, calibrated *whens*. Reason says they died

from time and deviation. That vision can't be trusted:
the octant's sightline, quivered by an eyelash,

the compass needle, vised by dust, sunlight's runway
on the water, even the slack-weave net of longitude

cast to gather time and space, a few salt stars,
the mackerel sky. The folly of its dateline
throws travelers into yesterday, and so the snub-nose plane
quickly crossed into the past, and stalled, and sank,

the theories say, one hour *before* departure.

Reason asks for grace with time, a little latitude
that lets a dateline shiver at the intervals of loss
and gain. As vision does, within
those intervals—and though it can't be trusted, still
it circles back, time and time again:

the black Pacific closing over them. And then,
the click of glasses, orange and radiant.

Grand Forks

1997

An arc of pips across a playboard's field
tightens, then, in the Chinese game of Go,
curls back to weave a noose, a circle closing, closed.

Surrounded, one surrenders. Blindsided,
collared from behind. Then silence, or so
my friends revealed, the arc across their patchwork fields

not pips, but flood. The dikes collapsed, they said;
the river, daily, swelled. Then *pastures* rose,
as earth's dark water table—brimful—spilled, and closed

behind their backs, the chaff-filled water red
with silt, with coulees, creeks, a russet snow,
all merging from behind. Then through the bay-bright fields

a dorsal silence came. And, turning, filled
the sunken streets, the fallen dikes, the slow,
ice-gripped periphery where frozen cattle closed

across their frozen likenesses. Mirrored,
as when the Northern Lights began, their glow
was mirrored, green to green, across the flooded fields—
like haunted arcs of spring, one circle closing, closed.

The Circus Riders

●℮ಿ℀— MARC CHAGALL, 1969

Sly-eyed and weightless, my violet rooster
quietly crosses a tent's blue dome.
He is buoyant, inverted, a migrating, wattled chandelier

that blinks from a ceiling's cool expanse
as the astronauts do—now one, now two, now three—
in orbit past a camera lens. While I dapple his beak
with a palette knife—and the acrobat's tights,
and the gallery's blue curve—the astronauts

crackle from space, their silver suits
shining like herring brine. They tell me the stars,
ungrated by atmosphere, do not twinkle at all, but
glow in their slow orbs, like shells on a black beach.
Now and then, through a tiny, waste-water door,

a galaxy of urine rolls, each oval drop bloated,
indistinguishable, they say, from the stars.
And the sextant quivers through this human heaven!

●℮ಿ℀—

On a sky of henna and cypress green,
a purple moon lingers. I placed to its left
a grandfather clock, massive, floating up
from a village's peaked roofs, then tilting to gravity's arc.
With its walls and weightless precision, my clock

seems a spacecraft's twin, a few seconds—
lacquered to history—pressed to the crystal
like faces. When I was ten, the Russian woods held a haze
of white birches. Specters, I thought, that sidestroked
at night past my open window, their leafy hoods
rattling. And now they are back,

waving from space, humming Dvořák's minor keys—
the plaintive A's, the pensive E's—their world
a little bead of sound
in that vast, unbroken soundlessness. A little
glint, and rhythmic tick.

●◦◦—

No chemist, Delacroix!
His paints will not dry.
Over time, the horse heads would sag into roan melons,
the portraits scowl, the lions relax their clenched jaws,

were they not, on alternate years, hung upside down
on their brass hooks—walls of inverted Delacroixs

regaining their borders, seeping back into neck scarves
and bridles, as my specters seeped back into
birch leaves. On those lessening nights, I watched

my father, asleep in his slim bed. His shoulders
and chest. Now and then, the glisten of herring scales
at his wrists. Head back, his full beard pointed toward
Mars, he seemed balanced there between death
and exertion, while the tannery's smells—sharp
as the odors of art—swept over us, and its
paddocked cattle, in the frail balance
of their own hours, shifted and lowed.

So this was the body
emptied. Exhausted. I stood between
terror and splendor as time and what must be
the soul—as the day and the day's morning—
seeped back to him.

●℮℘o—

And so they are circling back, the riders,
a talc of pumice on their boot soles.
When it all began, they said, and gravity
first dropped its grip, an effluvium of parts
flew up, hidden from brooms and the vacuum:
. . .

a curl of ash, a comb's black tooth, one slender
strip of cellophane, and what must have stung
those steady hearts: a single, silver screw—

now vertical, now cocked, now looping slowly
past each troubled face. . . . But nothing failed,
and so they've turned, the fire of their engines

a violet-feathered plume. My acrobat kicks up
one weightless leg. And holds. Across the room
a green tea brews. Their pulses
must have lurched, then stalled—the screw, the soft,
undissipated curl of ash: their craft
was crafted, and, crafted, flawed!

I see them in their silver suits, stunned
to numbness, as, looping slowly by, two sets
of pale, concentric rings fused nothing
more than air and human quickening.

An eye-blink's time, perhaps, before they felt
themselves return: that wash of rhythmic strokes,
that hum.

But that was their
moment, their wonder.

I tremble before my own heart.